felt
button
bead

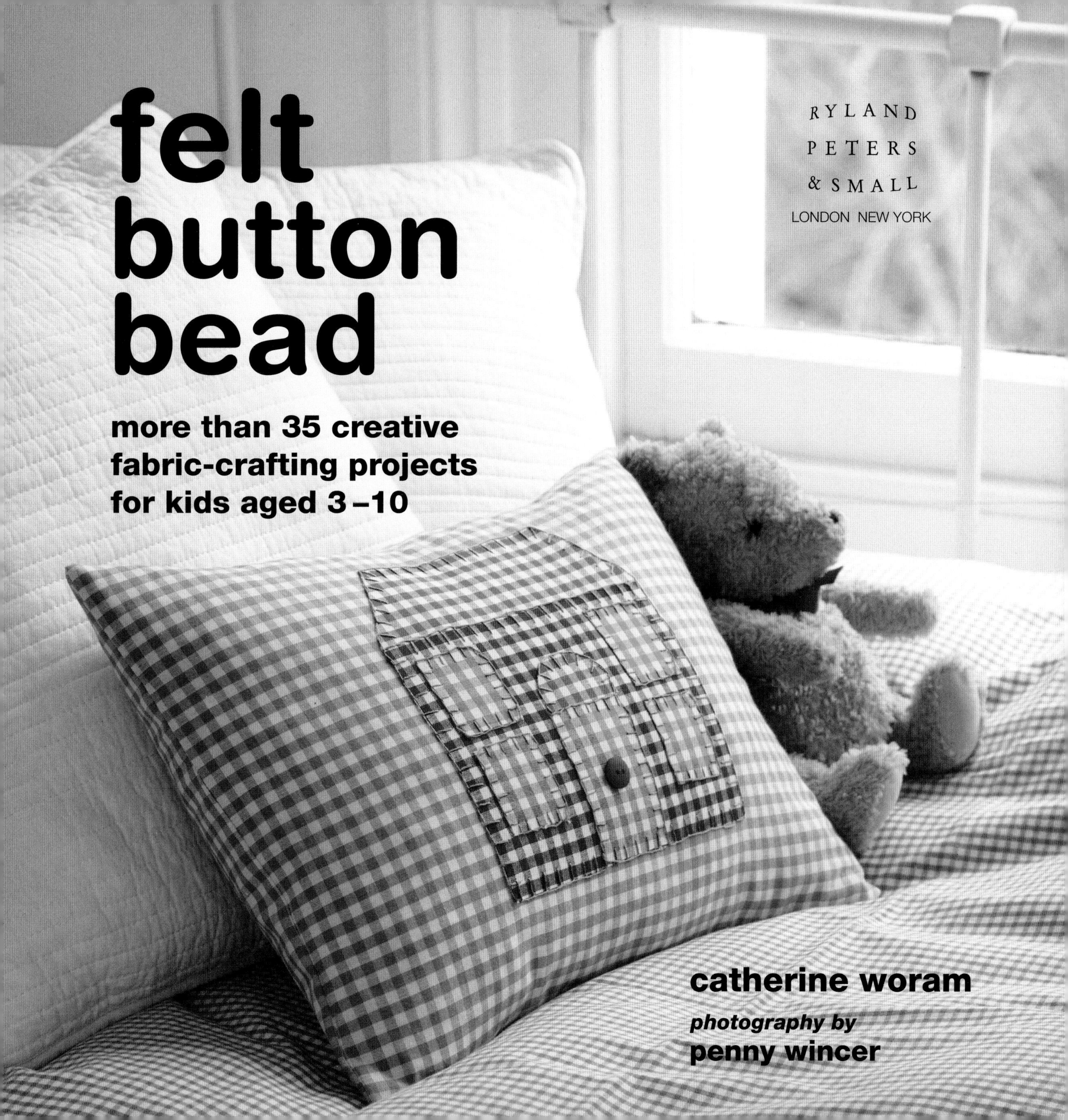

felt
button
bead

**more than 35 creative
fabric-crafting projects
for kids aged 3–10**

RYLAND
PETERS
& SMALL
LONDON NEW YORK

catherine woram

photography by
penny wincer

Senior designer Sonya Nathoo
Commissioning editor Annabel Morgan
Location research Jess Walton
Production Toby Marshall
Art director Leslie Harrington
Publishing director Alison Starling

Stylist Catherine Woram

First published in 2011
by Ryland Peters & Small
20–21 Jockey's Fields
London WC1R 4BW
and
519 Broadway, 5th Floor
New York, NY 10012
www.rylandpeters.com

10 9 8 7 6 5 4 3 2 1

Text, design and photographs
© Ryland Peters & Small 2011

ISBN: 978-1-84975-113-1

A CIP record for this book is available from the
British Library.

Library of Congress Cataloging-in-Publication
Data has been applied for.

Printed and bound in China.

contents

introduction

Felt Button Bead contains a selection of fun fabric crafting projects, ranging from funky clothes and accessories to pretty gift ideas. I hope that adults and kids alike will find the projects appealing and inspiring. Most of them can be carried out by a child with little or no adult assistance, but an adult should always supervise younger children when they are using scissors or working with heat or sharp objects.

Each project is accompanied by a series of simple step-by-step photographs that are easy to follow. You will also find a Techniques section at the back of the book (see pages 114–117) that explains the simple stitches used in many of the projects. It's a good idea to start off by practising some of these stitches before starting on the projects themselves. All kids will benefit from a basic knowledge of sewing. It's a practical skill that will serve them into adulthood – who knows when a button will fall off or a hem come down?

Both my daughters (now aged 12 and 13) are very good at sewing, although I have not formally taught them. They have picked it up by watching me and have drawn inspiration from always having a sewing box full of fabrics, buttons and threads to hand. They have now progressed from small craft projects to customizing their own clothes to create outfits that are the envy of all their friends.

I do hope you will enjoy the projects in this book as much as we enjoyed creating and photographing them, and that your family and friends will appreciate being the recipients of many wonderful handmade objects and gifts!

toys
and
games

YOU WILL NEED:
paper • scissors • 1 sheet felt
• pencil • pinking shears •
needle • embroidery thread •
3-D fabric pen • wooden button
(2cm/¾in diameter) • felt glue •
5cm/2in rickrack braid • felt
scraps • knitting wool

draw template Photocopy the finger puppet template on page 120 and cut it out. Place the template on the back of the felt and draw round it twice with the pencil. Cut out the two shapes using pinking shears.

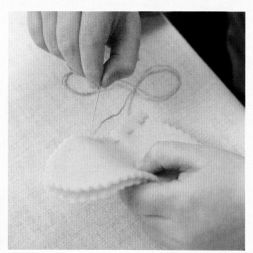

start sewing Thread the needle with embroidery thread and sew the two pieces of felt together using running stitch (see Techniques, page 116) and working approximately 3mm/⅛in in from the edges. Cast off securely to prevent the stitching from coming undone. Now use the 3-D fabric pens to draw a little face on the wooden button, using the two thread holes as eyes. Allow to dry completely.

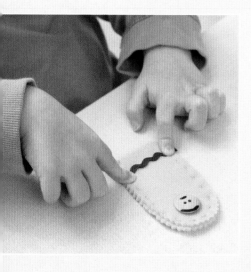

decorate puppet Glue the button face in place at the top of the finger puppet. Cut a length of rickrack to fit the bottom edge of the puppet and glue it onto the felt. Use the 3-D pen to draw on more hair, buttons and other details as desired.

finishing Cut out a bow-tie shape from a scrap of felt and glue it to the front of the finger puppet to finish. Why not create a whole family of puppets using the same template and add plaits made from knitting wool and other felt accessories?

finger puppets

These cute finger puppets are made from coloured felt and decorated with buttons, scraps of rickrack and braid. The sewing is very simple so this is an ideal project for younger crafters.

cuddly bear

This cute bear is made from a soft wool fabric
and sewn together using simple blanket stitch.
See the following pages to make a pretty
dress for your bear.

YOU WILL NEED:

paper • scissors • 25 x 60cm/
10 x 24in wool fabric or felt
• pins • needle • embroidery
thread in 2 different colours
• 4 buttons (about 1cm/⅛in
diameter) • polyester toy
stuffing • 40cm/16in ribbon
(about 1cm/⅛in wide)

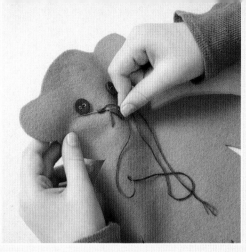

create template Photocopy the
teddy template on page 118 and cut it
out. Fold the fabric in half, pin the template
to the fabric and carefully cut out around
it so you have two teddy shapes. Take
one of the body shapes, thread the
needle with embroidery thread and stitch
the buttons in position as shown on the
template. Work the nose in small straight
stitches just below the eyes.

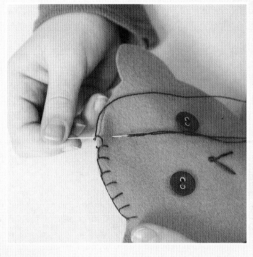

start stitching Thread the needle with the different-coloured
embroidery thread. Position the two pieces of fabric with wrong
sides together (pin them together if necessary) and begin stitching
them together all the way around the edges using blanket stitch
(see Techniques, page 114). The stitches should be about 5mm/¼in
apart. Remember to leave an opening of approximately 5cm/2in, so
you can stuff the bear.

stuff bear Insert the stuffing into the bear through the opening. Take small pieces
of stuffing and use the end of a paintbrush or a knitting needle to push them firmly down
to the very bottom of the bear's legs and arms. Insert enough stuffing so that the toy is
plump and easy to hold but not too firm or overstuffed.

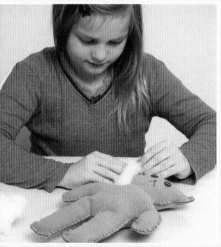

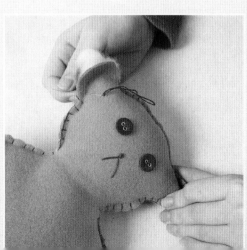

finishing Once the bear is stuffed, sew
the opening closed using blanket stitch.
Tie the ribbon around the bear's neck and
into a bow. Cut the ribbon ends on the
diagonal to prevent them from fraying.
Sew two more buttons to the front of the
bear just below the neck to finish.

YOU WILL NEED:

22 x 36 cm/9 x 14in cotton fabric • scissors • needle • matching sewing thread • safety pin • 20cm/8in elastic • 25cm/10in ribbon (1cm/½in wide)

cut out Fold the fabric in half with short end to short end then cut along the fold to give you two rectangles measuring 22 x 18cm/9 x 7in. Place them together with right sides facing and sew along the two long sides of the fabric using running stitch (see Techniques, page 116). Stop approximately 10cm/4in away from one short end to leave space for the armholes.

sew sides together You will now have a tube of fabric. At the bottom edge, fold in a 1cm/½in hem and use running stitch to sew it in place. Now, working at the top of the dress where the side seams end, neatly fold the raw edges in 1cm/½in to the wrong side and use running stitch to sew them in place.

make casing At the top of the dress, fold in a 2cm/¾in hem to the wrong side of the fabric and use running stitch to sew in place. This will form the casing for the elastic, so leave the ends open. Attach the safety pin to one end of the elastic and insert it into one opening. Chase it through the casing and out the other. Gather the elastic so that it fits the neck of the bear, trim the ends and sew them together securely.

finishing Put the dress on the bear and sew together the casing at the shoulders, taking care not to stitch through the elastic at the same time. Tie the ribbon into a bow, trim the ends on the diagonal to prevent them from fraying, and stitch the bow to the front of the dress.

bear's best dress

Make your cuddly bear this simple dress in a pretty floral fabric decorated with a pretty bow.

felt mp3 cover

This cute little mp3 cover is made from felt and is decorated with googly eyes and a fun pompom nose. Why not make several in different colours and give them to friends as presents for birthdays or at Christmas?

YOU WILL NEED:
paper • scissors • 2 sheets coloured felt • pins • pen • contrasting coloured embroidery thread • needle • felt glue • small pompom nose • 2 googly eyes

create template Photocopy the template on page 118 and cut it out. Place the template on the back of one piece of felt and draw around it. Repeat with the second piece of felt. Cut out the two pieces. Take one piece of felt (this will be the back). Punch a small hole (for the wires) at the bottom then cut along the line shown on the template (this slit will be the opening for the mp3 player).

start sewing Carefully lining up all the edges, place the two back pieces of the case on top of the front piece with wrong sides together. Pin them together if necessary. Thread the needle with a single strand of embroidery thread and begin stitching around the edge using blanket stitch (see Techniques, page 114). The stitches should be about 3mm/⅛in apart. As you sew, make a few additional stitches to reinforce the sides of the cut edges of the opening where the mp3 player will be inserted.

stick on nose On the front of the cover, use simple straight stitches to work two 'whiskers' about a third of the way down from the top. Then apply a dab of felt glue to the pompom for the nose and stick it firmly in place. Allow the glue to dry.

finishing Apply a dab of glue to the back of each of the googly eyes and stick them one either side and slightly above the pompom nose. Allow the glue to dry completely before using your case.

YOU WILL NEED:

old sock without any holes
• sewing thread • needle •
3 buttons • contrasting
coloured embroidery thread
• polyester toy stuffing • double
knitting wool for hair • scissors

sew on buttons Take the sock
and stitch the first button approximately
2cm/¾in above the heel to form a nose.
For the eyes, sew on two more buttons
about 3cm/1¼in above this and roughly
2cm/¾in apart.

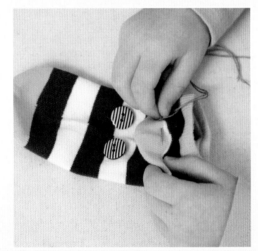

stitch on mouth Use your fingers to fold the heel of the
sock so it forms a mouth shape. Now stitch along the inside
edge of the heel using running stitch (see Techniques, page 116).
Use brightly coloured thread to make a feature of the mouth.

stuff sock Stuff the sock, pushing in small pieces of stuffing at a time. You may need
to use a knitting needle or paintbrush to push the stuffing to the end of the sock. Insert
enough stuffing so the toy is plump and easy to hold. When you have finished, use
whipstitch (see Techniques, page 116) to sew the bottom of the sock closed.

add hair Cut about 20 strands of wool,
each measuring 10cm/4in long, and use
one of the lengths to firmly tie the strands
together in the middle. Now stitch the mop
of hair to the top of the sock toy using
a needle and embroidery thread and
pushing the thread through the knot
that holds the hair together.

crazy sock creatures

Both boys and girls will love these characterful toys made from brightly coloured and boldly patterned old socks. Decorate them with buttons and make their tufty hair from a handful of wool strands.

peg dolly

This dainty dolly and her friend were made using traditional wooden clothes pegs and are dressed in pretty cotton frocks decorated with rickrack. They are the perfect size for dolls houses, so you could make a family of them.

YOU WILL NEED:

wooden peg • 3-D fabric paint in red and black • red paint for shoes • fine paintbrush • paper • scissors • pencil • scraps of floral fabric for dress • 20cm/8in narrow rickrack • small flower motif for hat • PVA/white glue • pinking shears

paint on hair Use the black fabric pen for the doll's hair and eyes. Paint on the hair quite thickly but not so much that the paint drips. Stand the peg upright in a small pot or jar while the paint dries.

draw on face Carefully draw two dots for the eyes using the black 3-D fabric pen and a small line for the doll's mouth using the red pen. Stand in a pot to dry, as before.

paint shoes Pour a small amount of the red paint onto a plate and use a fine paintbrush to paint the 'shoes' on the bottom of the peg. Allow the paint to dry completely. You may need to apply a second coat for complete coverage.

cut out dress Photocopy the doll's dress template on page 120 and cut it out. Place the template on the wrong side of your piece of fabric and draw all the way around it with a pencil. Cut out the dress using a pair of pinking shears to prevent the fabric edges from fraying.

glue braid Cut a length of rickrack to the same width as the bottom of the dress. Apply a fine layer of glue in a line that follows the curve of the dress about 1cm/½in from the bottom. Carefully place the rickrack along this line and press it down firmly. Allow the glue to dry.

make sleeves Using pinking shears, cut two lengths of fabric measuring 4 x 4cm/1½ x 1½in. Fold the fabric four times so that the sleeve width is about 1cm/½in and apply glue to the inside of the fabric. Push the edges together and allow the glue to dry completely.

attach dress Lay the fabric right side down on a flat surface and place the peg doll on top of the fabric with the neck of the peg in line with the top of the dress. Roll the fabric around the doll and put a dab of glue at the top to stick the dress to the doll's neck. Run a line of glue along the inside of the dress from the top to bottom and press the fabric down firmly. Allow the glue to dry completely.

finishing Use a dab of glue to attach one arm to each side of the dress and cut a small piece of rickrack to fit snugly round the neck of the peg doll. Glue this in place to cover the raw edges of the sleeves. Glue the embroidered flower motif to the top of the doll's head to finish.

dvd carry case

Make this cool DVD carrier using a ready-made case and decorate it with buttons and googly eyes plus a fun skull-and-crossbones motif. This is a no-sew project that's great for younger children.

YOU WILL NEED:

fusible web • small piece of fabric with skull-and-crossbones motif • pencil • scissors • round DVD case • 7-8 buttons in assorted designs or poppers • 5 googly eyes • PVA/white glue • 15cm/6in rickrack

make motif Ask an adult to help you iron the fusible web to the back of the skull-and-crossbones fabric. Let it cool. Draw a circle on the paper side of the fusible web (a lid would be a good template, or use a compass), making sure that the skull motif is positioned exactly in the middle of the circle.

cut out motif Use scissors to carefully cut out the circular motif. Peel off the backing paper and position the circle in the centre of the DVD case. Ask an adult to help you iron the motif in place, following the manufacturer's instructions, and allow to cool.

stick on buttons Glue your buttons, googly eyes and poppers at regular intervals around the edge of the case. Press each button down firmly with your finger to make sure they are securely in place. Allow the glue to dry completely.

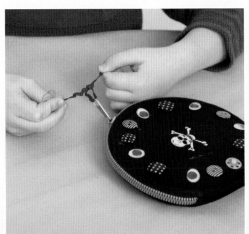

finishing Cut a length of rickrack about 15cm/6in long and thread it through the hole of the zipper. Tie the rickrack in a knot and pull the ends firmly to secure. Cut the ends of the rickrack on the diagonal to prevent them from fraying.

YOU WILL NEED:

45 x 45cm/18 x 18in square calico • masking tape • red fabric paint • stencil brush • pinking shears • paper • pencil • scissors • 1 sheet yellow felt • 1 sheet blue felt • 12 striped buttons (2cm/¾in diameter) • 12 spotted buttons (2cm/¾in diameter) • glue

attach masking tape Stick the first row of masking tape all along the straight edge of the fabric, about 1cm/½in in from the edge. Now stick down another strip of tape parallel with the first one but about 5cm/2in apart. Continue to stick down rows of masking tape until there are four parallel lines of tape in total.

mark out squares Next, stick down rows of masking tape running in the opposite direction at a 90° angle to the original taped rows, leaving 5cm/2in between each row as before. Continue to stick down masking tape until you have created another four parallel lines of masking tape.

start painting Once you have finished sticking down the rows of masking tape, a pattern of squares will be left exposed. Pour some fabric paint into a saucer and dip in the stencil brush. Use a piece of paper to blot any excess paint then paint the exposed squares using a brisk dabbing motion. Leave the paint to dry completely, or it may smudge when you remove the masking tape.

paint squares When the paint is completely dry, peel off the tape. Then carefully stick rows of masking tape over the rows of painted squares, creating another four lines of tape in each direction. A pattern of squares will be left exposed. Use the stencil brush and fabric paint to fill in all the remaining squares.

travel game

This fun draughts/checkers game is ideal for travel as it can be rolled up for easy packing and the felt and button pieces are lightweight too. It's a great no-sew project for anyone who loves painting and glueing.

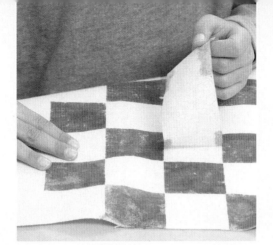

remove tape Once the paint is completely dry, carefully peel off the masking tape. There will be a red and white chequered pattern on the calico. Use pinking shears to trim the edges of the fabric to prevent it from fraying.

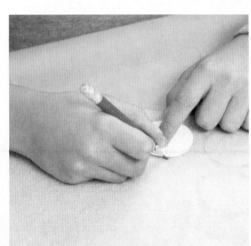

make pieces Photocopy the circle template on page 119 and cut it out. Place the template on the yellow felt and draw around it with a pencil. Continue until you have enough pieces. You will need twelve yellow and twelve turquoise circles in total, but you may also wish to make a few spare pieces.

cut out shapes Use scissors to carefully cut out the twenty-four circular shapes from the two different-coloured pieces of felt. Decide which type of button will go on which coloured circle.

glue on buttons Apply glue to the back of each button and press one button firmly to the centre of each felt circle. Allow the glue to dry completely. Keep the rolled-up board and pieces in a drawstring bag, ready for long journeys.

YOU WILL NEED:
36 x 40cm/14 x 16in fabric for the pillowcase • pinking shears • rickrack • pins • needle • thread • embroidered braid • polyester toy stuffing • 2 pieces fabric, each measuring 50 x 36cm/20 x 14in for the coverlet • 50 x 13cm/20 x 5in piece of gingham for the coverlet

start with pillowcase Using pinking shears, cut a piece of fabric measuring 36 x 40 cm/14 x 16in for the pillowcase. Fold in a 1cm/½in hem along one long 40cm/16in side and ask an adult to help you press it in place with a hot iron. Now pin the rickrack all along the folded edge, about 1cm/½in below the fold. Stitch in place using running stitch (see Techniques, page 116).

sew on braid Pin the braid to the front of the fabric, positioning it about 2cm/¾in below the line of rickrack. Stitch it to the fabric with a line of whipstitch (see Techniques, page 116) along both sides of the braid.

stitch pillowcase Fold the fabric in half with right sides facing, so that the braid and rickrack are on the inside. Line up all the edges and use running stitch to sew along the two open sides, leaving the rickrack edge open. Trim and notch the corners of the fabric and turn the pillowcase to the right side. Ask an adult to press it flat with a hot iron if necessary.

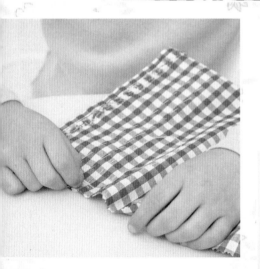

stuff pillowcase Push small pieces of polyester toy stuffing into the cushion until it is full. Insert enough stuffing so that the cushion is plump, but not overstuffed. To finish, sew the opening closed using whipstitch.

doll's bedding set

This pretty coverlet and pillowcase for a doll's bed are simple to make and very effective. We used contrasting fabric to line the quilt – a combination of spots, stripes and squares looks great – and added ribbon and rickrack to finish.

start coverlet Place one piece of fabric for the top of the coverlet on a flat surface. Now place the strip of gingham on top at one end, making sure all the raw edges are lined up. Pin the gingham to the striped fabric. Now use whipstitch to sew the embroidered braid along the bottom edge of the gingham to hide the raw edges. Stitch both sides of the braid.

sew on rickrack Using running stitch, stitch the rickrack onto the gingham fabric parallel to and about 2cm/¾in away from the embroidered braid. Ask an adult to help you press the braid and rickrack flat using a hot iron.

stitch coverlet together Place the striped fabric and the spotted lining fabric with right sides together and all raw edges lined up. Pin together then stitch all the way along three sides, leaving just the bottom edge open. Trim and notch the corners of the fabric and turn to the right side.

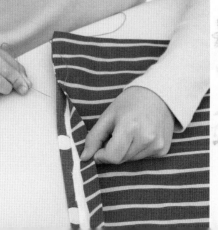

finishing Fold in a 2cm/¾in hem along the bottom and ask an adult to help you press it in place using a hot iron. To finish, use a line of whipstitch to sew the opening closed.

gifts

YOU WILL NEED:

plain notebook • bandana •
scissors • scarf • PVA/white
glue • embroidered initials

cut out fabric Open the notebook
out flat on the wrong side of the bandana.
Cut all the way around the book, allowing
a 3cm/1¼in margin around all edges. Now
close the book and place the spine in the
centre of the fabric with the bottom of the
book facing towards you. Cut two parallel
slits at the top and bottom of the spine.
Push these pieces of fabric inside the
spine and glue in place. Allow to dry.

start sticking To glue the bandana inside the notebook, place
the front cover flat and rest the other part of the book against your
body while you work. Neatly fold the fabric to the inside along the
long outside edge of the book and glue it in position.

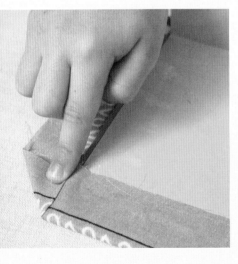

fold corners When the outside edge has dried, fold the corners of the fabric neatly
towards the inside of the book then turn in the fabric at the top and bottom edges and
glue it in place. Repeat the glueing process at the back of the book and let it dry.

finishing Now stick one or two
embroidered initials on the front of the
book. Allow the glue to dry completely.

bandana notebook

I used colourful bandana scarves to make these covered notebooks. To personalize them, stick pretty embroidered initials to front of the notebook.

patchwork cushion

This fun cushion is made from colourful fabric squares. It's a great way of recycling fabric scraps or old clothes you have grown out of. Finished with a pretty flower motif, it makes a great gift for family or friends.

YOU WILL NEED:

paper • scissors • pins
• assorted fabric squares
measuring at least 11 x 11cm/
4½ x 4½in each • needle •
thread • 2 rectangles of fabric,
each measuring 40 x 25cm/
16 x 10in for back • flower
motif • small bead • 40 x 40cm/
16 x 16in square cushion pad

cut out squares On a piece of paper, draw a square measuring 11 x 11cm/4½ x 4½in and cut it out. This is your patchwork template. Pin the square onto the back of the fabric pieces and cut out 16 squares.

stitch together Place two squares together with right sides facing. Pin if necessary. Now stitch the two squares together along one side, using a small running stitch (see Techniques, page 116) and working 5mm/¼in from the raw edges. You could use back stitch (see Techniques, page 116) for a stronger finish, although it will take more time.

clip edges and press When you have sewn together a strip of four patches, trim and notch the seams and ask an adult to help you press them flat using a hot iron. Put this strip to one side. Continue sewing patches together with right sides facing until you have four strips of four patches each.

continue sewing Place two strips together with right sides facing. Pin if necessary. Stitch together along one long side of each strip using running stitch, 5mm/¼in from the edges. Repeat until all four strips have been attached and you have a piece of patchwork with 16 squares in total. Ask an adult to help you press the seams with an iron.

cut out backing fabric From the backing fabric, cut two rectangles measuring 40 x 25cm/16 x 10in. Place them together with right sides facing and pin in place if necessary. Working on one long (40cm/16in) edge, stitch in about 5cm/2in from the edge, using back stitch and sewing about 3cm/1¼in from the raw edge. Cast off securely.

stitch backing together Now stitch inwards from the other end of the long edge for about 5cm/2in, again using back stitch. Cast off securely. There will now be a 30cm/12in gap in the middle of your stitching which forms the opening through which to insert the cushion. Open the fabric out and ask an adult to help you press the seam flat using a hot iron.

stitch flower Thread the needle and stitch the flower motif to one corner of the cushion front. Sew a bead to the middle of the flower for decoration.

stitch cushion together Place the patchwork and back section together with right sides facing. Using back stitch, sew around all four edges, about 1cm/½in from the edge. Turn the cover right side out. Insert the cushion pad and stitch the opening closed using whipstitch (see Techniques, page 116).

handy shopper

This useful shopping bag makes a great gift for Mother's Day or a grandparent. Made from cream calico, it is stencilled with a cheerful boat motif and trimmed with lengths of colourful rickrack. You could also stencil on your initials to personalize the bag.

YOU WILL NEED:

2 pieces of calico each measuring 52 x 40cm/21 x 16in • pinking shears • 80cm/32in red rickrack • 80cm/32in green rickrack • needle • thread • boat stencil • red and blue fabric paint • stencil brush • masking tape • embroidery thread • 80cm/32in cream cotton ribbon for handles • 80cm/32in jumbo rickrack

cut out fabric Take the two pieces of fabric measuring 52 x 40cm/21 x 16in and trim the edges using pinking shears to prevent them from fraying.

sew on rickrack Cut the two lengths of rickrack in half, so you have four lengths in total. Take one of the pieces of calico. This will be the front of the bag. Pin a length of rickrack across the calico, parallel to one of the shorter edges and about 5cm/2in in from the edge of the fabric. Stitch the rickrack in place using running stitch (see Techniques, page 116). Next, pin then stitch the second row of rickrack in place about 3cm/1¼in above this. Repeat at the other end of the fabric, stitching the first row of rickrack about 8cm/3in in from the raw edge and the second row about 3cm/1¼in above the first.

stencil design on bag Place the stencil in the centre of the front fabric piece, spaced evenly between the rows of rickrack. Use masking tape to hold the corners in place. Dip the stencil brush in the fabric paint and blot any excess paint on a piece of kitchen paper so that the brush is fairly dry. Fill in the waves motif with blue paint, using a dabbing motion. Leave the paint to dry completely.

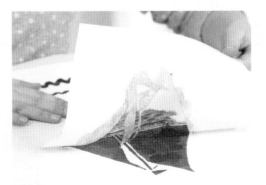

remove stencil When the blue paint is completely dry, cover it with masking tape. Now use the red fabric paint to fill in the rest of the stencil detail. Leave to dry. When the paint is completely dry, carefully peel off the stencil to reveal the motif.

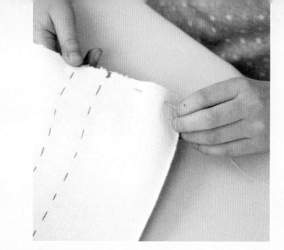

stitch bag together Pin the two pieces of calico together with right sides facing, so the stencil and rickrack trim are on the inside. Stitch the two long sides and one short side of the bag together using back stitch (see Techniques, page 116) and strong sewing thread (use buttonhole thread, if possible). Leave the top edge of the bag open.

sew top hem Fold 3cm/1¼in of the top edge of the bag to the inside and ask an adult to help you press the hem flat using a hot iron. Stitch the hem in place using running stitch and contrasting coloured embroidery thread for a decorative effect.

make handles Lay a row of jumbo rickrack along the centre of each 40cm/16in piece of handle and pin it in place. Stitch the rickrack to the first handle piece using running stitch. Repeat for the second handle.

finishing Stitch the handles to the front and back of the bag about 12cm/5in in from the side seams and use three large cross stitches to hold them securely in place. You may wish to make the handles stronger by stitching around them on the inside using whipstitch (see Techniques, page 116) and cream sewing thread.

handprint kitchen towel

This fun project will appeal to younger crafters who like getting their hands messy! You could use a shop-bought kitchen towel to make the project even easier for young children.

YOU WILL NEED:

piece of gingham fabric
measuring 40 x 70cm/16 x 28in
• scissors • contrast
embroidery thread • needle
• coloured fabric paint •
paintbrush or stencil brush

cut out fabric Cut a piece of gingham measuring 40 x 70cm/16 x 28in and try to use the fabric selvedge for the bottom hem. This saves on hemming and adds a decorative effect. Fold in a 1cm/½in hem to the wrong side around the three remaining raw edges and stitch in place using running stitch (see Techniques, page 116).

apply paint to hands Dip the brush in the fabric paint and apply it to one of the child's hands, making sure to cover the palm and fingers completely. Make sure the paint is not too thick. Keep a damp cloth close by in case of accidents.

start printing Encourage the child to press his or her painted hand down firmly on the kitchen towel with fingers slightly splayed to create the handprint. Lift the hand up carefully to avoid smudging the paint. Allow to dry completely. You may have to apply more paint to the hand and print it twice for full coverage.

finishing Wash the child's hand and apply a different colour paint to the child's palm. Now repeat the printing process and leave the paint to dry completely. Ask an adult to help you iron the kitchen towel to seal the fabric paint, following the manufacturer's instructions.

YOU WILL NEED:

paper • scissors • 1 piece red felt 43 x 30cm/17 x 12in • 1 piece blue felt 43 x 30cm/ 17 x 12in • 1 smaller piece red felt 43 x 15cm/17 x 6in • 20 x 20cm/8 x 8in gingham • fusible web • pencil • contrasting coloured embroidery thread • pinking shears • 60cm/24in gingham ribbon (2cm/¾in wide)

create template Photocopy the slanted pocket template on page 120 and cut out. Then cut out two pieces of felt measuring 43 x 30cm/17 x 12in, one from blue felt and one from red felt. Pin the pocket template on to the smaller 43 x 15cm/17 x 6in piece of red felt and cut all the way around it.

create initial Iron the fusible web to the back of the gingham fabric and leave it to cool. Draw your chosen initial on a piece of paper then cut it out to use as a template. Place the initial template on the paper side of the fusible web and draw all the way around it. Remember that you will need to reverse non-symmetrical initials when drawing them on the back of fabric.

cut out initial Carefully cut out the initial. Peel off the backing paper and position it on the front of the larger red felt rectangle in the front bottom corner. This will be the front of the tool wrap. Ask an adult to help you use a hot iron to fix in place, following the manufacturer's instructions. Let it cool.

start blanket stitch Thread a needle with embroidery thread and work blanket stitch (see Techniques, page 114) all the way around the initial. The stitches should be about 5mm/¼in apart. Cast off securely when you have finished.

felt tool wrap

A great gift for Father's Day, this colourful and practical felt tool wrap features an appliquéd gingham initial and gingham ribbon ties. You could also make it in a strong fabric such as denim – try using the bottom of an old pair of adult jeans.

stitch sections Place the blue felt fabric on a flat surface. Place the red pocket section on top, lining up the bottom and side edges. Pin in position if required. Now stitch six lines of running stitch at regularly spaced intervals to attach the pocket to the felt. These will create seven pockets for the tools.

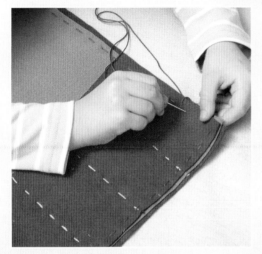

stitch layers together Next lay the blue fabric plus pocket on top of the main red fabric section with wrong sides of the fabric facing and use running stitch (see Techniques, page 116) to sew around all four edges, stitching approximately 1cm/½in from the edge of the felt.

trim edges When you have finished sewing the felt together, use pinking shears to trim all four edges of the fabric for a decorative effect. Be careful not to cut through any of your stitching.

stitch ribbon tie Measure 20cm/8in in from the end of the ribbon and make a fold. Stitch the fold to the front of the tool wrap on the inside using whipstitch (see Techniques, page 116). The ribbon should be positioned about halfway between the top and bottom of the wrap.

YOU WILL NEED:

50 x 70cm/20 x 28in stiff cardboard • 50 x 70cm/20 x 28in sheet of thin foam • star-print cotton fabric 60 x 80cm/ 24 x 32in • pinking shears • 6m/20ft gingham ribbon (1cm/½in wide) • drawing pins • strong glue

cover board Cut a piece of cardboard and a piece of thin foam measuring 50 x 70cm/20 x 28in, cutting the edges on a gentle curve. Place the fabric on a flat surface, wrong side up. Position the foam on top and the board on top of that and trim the edges of the fabric so there is an overlap of about 4cm/1½in all round. Use pinking shears to prevent the edges from fraying.

position ribbons Fold the fabric to the back of the board, pulling it taut so there are no wrinkles. Glue the fabric in place around all four edges. Allow to dry. Take the ribbon and cut four pieces that are long enough to run diagonally across the board at evenly spaced intervals of about 15cm/6in. Repeat, using four more ribbon lengths to cross over the first parallel lines and create a diamond pattern. Allow a margin of about 4cm/1½in at each end of the ribbon so you can glue it to the back of the board.

attach pins Push a drawing pin into the centre of each ribbon cross and press down firmly. Repeat until you have pushed a drawing pin into every ribbon cross.

finishing Turn the board over and pull the ribbon ends to the back. Apply glue to each ribbon end to secure it in position. Allow the glue to dry completely.

bulletin board

This practical bulletin board is made using a piece of stiff cardboard and bright and cheerful star-print cotton. Make one to match the fabrics in your bedroom for extra effect.

cross-stitch card

These dainty cards make the perfect Mother's Day or thank-you card. Decorated with tiny cross stitch and finished with a button, they could also be framed to create a long-lasting memento.

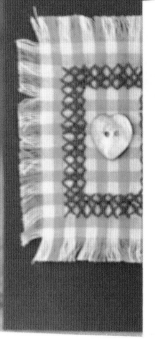

YOU WILL NEED:

30 x 30cm/12 x 12in gingham fabric • embroidery hoop • needle • contrast embroidery thread • scissors • strong glue • blank folded card • pretty button (about 2cm/¾in diameter)

begin stitching Place the gingham fabric in the embroidery hoop and stretch it until it is taut. Begin working the cross stitches (see Techniques, page 115). Use the gingham squares as a guide and stitch a square made up of three rows of eleven stitches each. This will leave a blank square of fabric in the middle for the button.

cut out fabric Remove the embroidery hoop and ask an adult to help you press the back of the fabric flat using a hot iron. Trim the fabric into a square leaving a margin of four gingham checks around each side of the cross-stitched square.

fray edges Start pulling the loose threads of the gingham gently away from the fabric to create a frayed effect. Continue to pull away the threads until you have frayed two gingham checks on each side of the square.

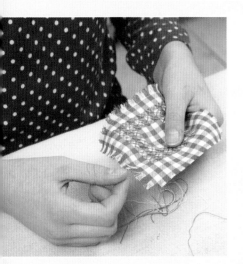

finishing Apply glue to the back of the fabric and stick the gingham square to the centre of the blank card. Press firmly to stick it in place. Glue a button to the centre of the gingham fabric to finish.

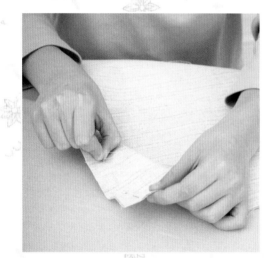

YOU WILL NEED:

paper • scissors • 1.2m/4ft fabric (137cm/54in wide) • needle • thread • 40cm/16in braid (1cm/½in wide) • 40cm/16in rickrack • 3 buttons (about 2cm/¾in diameter) • 3 felt flower motifs • small wooden clothes hanger

create template Photocopy the peg bag templates on pages 122–123 and cut them out. Fold the fabric in half with wrong sides together. Place the top flap section of the bag on the fabric so the straight edge lines up with the fold. Cut around the template. Now unfold the fabric, pin the main body template to it, draw around the template twice and cut out two body sections.

stitch together Place the two parts of the body section with right sides are facing. Now stitch together the two back sections of fabric along the short straight edge using back stitch (see Techniques, page 116). Turn over the seam and press flat.

sew on braid Take the top flap section of the peg bag and place it on a flat surface. Position the braid on the top section of the bag about 2cm/¾in above the fold in the fabric. Stitch the braid to the fabric with a line of whipstitch (see Techniques, page 116) along both sides of the braid and stitching through both layers of fabric.

stitch on decorations Sew the buttons and flowers to the main body of the bag. Stitch them in place along the edge of the bag, about 3cm/1¼in from the edge of the fabric. Sew the rickrack about 20cm/8in below this using running stitch (see Techniques, page 116).

peg bag with hanger

This traditional peg bag would make a pretty addition to any kitchen or laundry room, as well as a delightful and welcome gift.

stitch together With right sides facing, pin the top flap to the top of the body section, lining up the top curved edge and the sides. Now fold up the bottom edge of the body section and bring it up to meet the bottom of the top flap. Pin in place and sew along the top curved edge and the two sides, using back stitch. Leave an opening of about 2cm/¾in at the centre of the curved edge to insert the hanger.

trim edges Trim and notch the edges of the fabric at the corners and along the curved top edge of the peg bag. This will help the fabric to lie smoothly once it is turned to the right side. Carefully notch the opening at the middle of the top flap to make it easier to insert the hanger.

turn right side out Turn the peg bag to the right side and use the ends of scissors or a knitting needle to gently push the corners of the fabric out. Ask an adult to help you press the fabric with a hot iron to smooth out any creases.

finishing Insert the hanger inside the peg bag and push the metal hook of the hanger through the opening at the top of the curved edge. Manipulate the fabric so that it hangs smoothly on both sides from the edges of the wooden hanger.

YOU WILL NEED:

paper • scissors • fusible web
• pencil • 40 x 80cm/16 x 32in
gingham fabric • additional
gingham scraps for house
and doors/windows • needle
• sewing thread • buttons •
30 x 40cm/12 x 16in cushion
pad • ribbon • contrast
embroidery thread • 40cm/16in
ribbon (2cm/¾in wide)

create templates Photocopy the house, roof, window and door templates on page 120 and cut them out. Ask an adult to help you iron the fusible web onto the back of the scraps of gingham fabric, then allow the fabric to cool.

cut out house Place the templates on the paper side of the fusible web, draw around them in pencil and cut out the shapes. From the gingham fabric, cut one rectangle for the cushion front measuring 33 x 43cm/13 x 17in and two rectangles for the cushion back measuring 33 x 24cm/13 x 9½in. Take the larger piece of gingham (the cushion front) and place the house and roof shapes with the windows and doors on top. Lay a teatowel over the shapes and ask an adult to help you iron them in place, following the manufacturer's instructions.

start blanket stitch Leave the fabric to cool down completely. Thread the needle with embroidery thread and begin working blanket stitch (see Techniques, page 114) all around the outlines of the house and roof. Cast off your sewing securely to prevent the stitches coming undone.

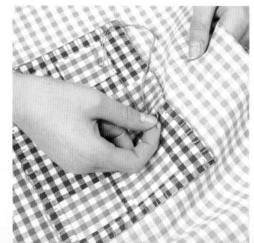

continue stitching Continue to blanket stitch around the door and then the windows. When you have finished sewing, ask an adult to help you iron the stitching on the reverse side of the fabric and then leave it to cool.

appliqué cushion

This cute gingham cushion with its appliquéd house motif worked in blanket stitch would make a great housewarming gift for someone special!

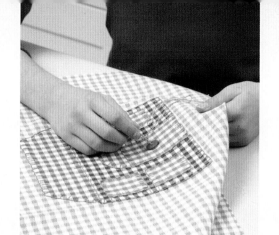

sew on button Place the button in the centre of the door on the front of the cushion and securely stitch in place.

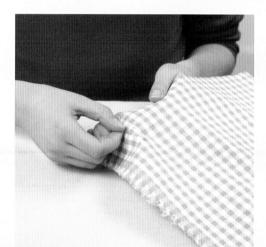

stitch back section Thread the needle with sewing thread. Place the two back sections of the cushion cover with right sides facing and pin in place if necessary. Working on one long edge, stitch in about 5cm/2in from the end, using back stitch and sewing about 3cm/1¼in from the raw edge. Now stitch inwards from the other end for about 5cm/2in, again using back stitch. Cast off securely. There will now be a gap in the middle of your stitching which forms the opening for the cushion pad.

stitch cover together Ask an adult to help you press the seam flat using a hot iron. Now place the front and back sections of the cushion together with right sides facing. Pin in place if necessary. Stitch around the four sides using back stitch (see Techniques, page 116). Notch the corners and turn the cover to the right side.

finishing Cut the ribbon into two 20cm/8in lengths and use whipstitch to attach one end of each piece to each side of the opening at the back of the cushion. These ties will hold the opening closed. Trim the ends of the ribbon on the diagonal to prevent them from fraying.

YOU WILL NEED:

paper • scissors • pins • 1 sheet felt for egg cosy • 1 sheet contrast felt for flower • needle • sewing thread • felt glue • embroidery thread • scissors • small pompom

create templates Photocopy the flower and egg cosy templates on page 118 and cut them out. Pin the petal template to the back of the felt and draw round it six times then cut out the six petals. Arrange them in a circle and begin sewing along the inner straight edge in a small running stitch (see Techniques, page 116). When you have finished sewing, pull gently on the running stitch so that the petals form a flower shape.

sew egg cosy Place the egg cosy template on the felt and draw around it twice. Cut out two cosy shapes. Place them together and blanket stitch around the curved edges, leaving the straight bottom edge open.

glue on flower Apply felt glue to the back of the flower and press it firmly down on the front of the egg cosy. Do not apply glue to the edges of the petals, as it will prevent them from standing out and creating a 3-D effect.

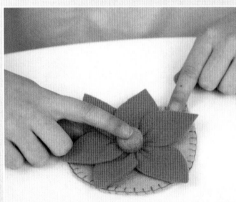

finishing Apply a dab of glue to the middle of the pompom and stick to the centre of the flower, pressing down firmly. Allow the glue to dry completely.

egg cosies

An ideal Easter gift or just a fun creative craft for the kitchen, these decorative egg cosies are simple to make and look very effective.

fleece blanket

Decorated with a fun boat motif, this fleece blanket is perfect for cuddling up in for a sleepover! Girls might like to make one from pink fleece, with a flower or heart motif.

YOU WILL NEED:

150cm/5ft fleece fabric
(150cm/5ft) wide • scissors •
boat motif (we cut ours from
printed cotton fabric) • fusible
web • contrastingly coloured
cotton embroidery thread
• double knitting wool
• large needle

cut out fabric Cut along the edges
of the fleece fabric to make sure they are
straight, and cut off the selvedge. Then
cut the corners of the blanket into a
gentle curve, which will make it easier
when you are stitching the edges.

cut out motif Iron the fusible web to the back of the fabric
and leave to cool. Cut out the boat motif, peel off the backing
paper and place the motif in one corner of the blanket. Cover with
a teatowel and ask an adult to help you press it with a hot iron.

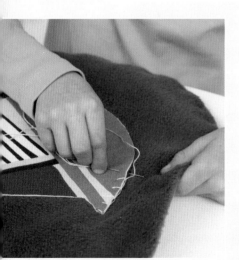

stitch motif Thread a needle with the embroidery thread and stitch around the boat
motif in blanket stitch (see Techniques, page 114). You may want to add some buttons
as extra decoration.

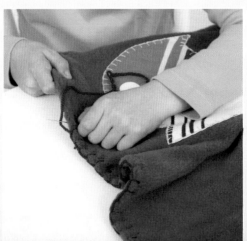

stitch blanket Fold in a 2cm/¾in
hem all the way around the blanket and
pin it in place ready for stitching. Thread
the needle with the knitting wool and
work blanket stitch around all four sides
of the blanket. The stitches should be
about 1–2cm/½–¾in apart.

clothing

YOU WILL NEED:

30 x 30cm/12 x 12in star-print fabric for guitar motif
• 30 x 30cm/12 x 12in fusible web • paper • pencil • scissors
• plain long-sleeved t-shirt
• Contrasting coloured embroidery thread • 3 assorted buttons (about 1cm/½in diameter) • sewing thread
• 3-D fabric paint

create template Ask an adult to help you iron the fusible web to the back of the star fabric and let it cool. Photocopy the template on page 119 and cut it out. Place the template on the paper side of the fusible web, draw around it and cut out the guitar shape. Peel off the backing paper and position the guitar in place on the front of the t-shirt. Ask an adult to help you iron it in place, following the manufacturer's instructions, and allow to cool.

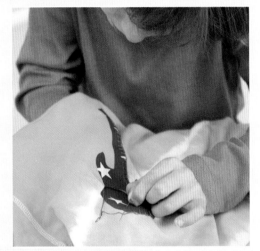

stitch around motif Thread the needle with the embroidery thread amd begin stitching all the way around the guitar motif in blanket stitch (see Techniques, page 114).

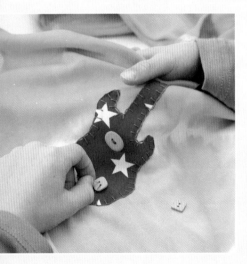

sew on buttons Stitch the three buttons on to the guitar using sewing thread. Make sure you cast off your sewing securely, so it does not come undone.

finishing Use the 3-D fabric pen to draw tiny dots along the handle of the guitar. Allow the paint to dry completely before wearing the t-shirt.

guitar t-shirt

Customize a plain t-shirt with this cool electric guitar motif decorated with blanket stitch and colourful buttons.

heart t-shirt

A simple heart-shaped motif in pretty floral fabric is decorated with tiny coloured buttons to create this appealing girl's t-shirt.

YOU WILL NEED:

20 x 20cm/8 x 8in floral
fabric for heart motif •
20 x 20cm/ 8 x 8in fusible web
• plain long-sleeved t-shirt
• scissors • pencil • contrasting
coloured embroidery thread
• needle • sewing thread •
5 small buttons (about
5mm/¼in diameter)

create template Ask an adult
to help you iron the fusible web to the
back of the floral fabric and allow to cool.
Photocopy the heart template on page
119 and cut out with scissors. Place the
template on the paper side of the fusible
web and draw around it in pencil.

cut out heart shape Cut out the heart. Peel off the
backing paper and position it in place on the front of the t-shirt.
Ask an adult to help you iron it in place, following the
manufacturer's instructions, and allow to cool.

stitch around motif Thread the needle with the embroidery thread and begin
stitching all the way around the heart motif in blanket stitch (see Techniques, page 114).
When you finish, cast off securely to prevent the stitching from coming undone.

finishing Use the sewing thread to sew
the five buttons to the heart. Make sure
you cast off your sewing securely, so it
does not come undone.

stitch rickrack Cut a length of rickrack to fit around the bottom of the first leg. Use running stitch (see Techniques, page 116) to sew it in place, stitching about 2.5cm/1in up from the hem. Trim the end of the rickrack, fold the raw edge to the inside and use whipstitch (see Techniques, page 116) to secure it in place. Now repeat with the other leg.

sew on beads Starting with the first leg, use a fine needle to sew the tiny beads all along the rickrack at 1cm/½in intervals. Repeat on the second leg.

attach more rickrack Use running stitch to attach a second row of rickrack braid all the way around the bottom of the first leg, sewing it in place about 2cm/¾in above the first row. Trim the end of the rickrack, fold the raw edge to the inside and use slipstitch to secure it in place.

finishing Working on the first leg, stitch the tiny buttons in a row at 1cm/½in intervals, sewing them about 2cm/¾in up from the rickrack. Make sure you cast off the stitching securely when you have finished. Repeat on the second leg of the jeans to finish.

decorated jeans

Update a plain pair of jeans with rows of colourful rickrack, tiny beads and colourful buttons to give them instant appeal. This would work equally well on plain coloured trousers too.

elasticated skirt

This pretty skirt is made from a cotton
fabric gathered with elastic and adorned
with fun appliquéd fabric flowers decorated
with blanket stitch and finished with buttons.

YOU WILL NEED:

35cm x 1m/14in x 3ft cotton fabric • pinking shears • scraps of fabric for flowers • fusible web • paper • scissors • pencil • embroidery thread • needle • sewing thread • 3 buttons (1cm/½in diameter) • 60cm/24in elastic (2.5cm/1in wide) • 20cm/8in ribbon (2cm/¾in wide) • safety pin

cut out skirt For the skirt, cut two pieces of fabric each measuring 35cm x 85cm/14 x 34in, using pinking shears to prevent the fabric edges from fraying. Place the two pieces together with right sides facing and stitch along one short end using back stitch (see Techniques, page 116) and working 1cm/½in from the raw edge.

create template Ask an adult to help you iron the fusible web to the back of the flower fabric and let it cool. Photocopy the flower template on page 119 and cut it out. Place the template on the paper side of the fusible web and draw around it three times to create three flower motifs. Peel off the backing paper and position the three flowers on the front of the skirt fabric. Ask an adult to help you iron them in place following the manufacturer's instructions and allow to cool.

stitch round on flowers Thread the needle with the embroidery thread and work blanket stitch (see Techniques, page 114) all the way around the flower motifs.

sew on buttons Once you have worked blanket stitch around all three of the flowers, sew a button to the middle of each flower. Make sure you cast off carefully so that the buttons are secure.

stitch side seams Fold the skirt fabric together with right sides facing. Use back stitch (see Techniques, page 116) to stitch together the short ends, working 1cm/½in from the raw edges. Notch the seam so it lies flat and ask an adult to help you to press open the seam using a hot iron.

sew hem and elastic casing Fold over the top and bottom edges of the fabric by 3cm/1¼in to form a hem at the bottom and a casing for the elastic at the top. Sew in place using small running stitches (see Techniques, page 116). Leave the ends of the casing open so you can insert the elastic.

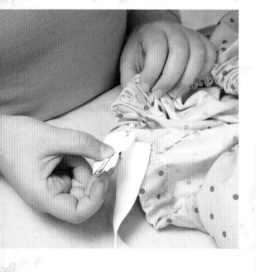

insert elastic Wrap the elastic around your waist until you find a length that feels comfortable. Cut the elastic to this length then attach the safety pin to one end. Insert the elastic into the casing through one opening. Chase the elastic all the way through the casing and out the other end. Remove the safety pin and securely stitch together the two ends of the elastic.

finishing Sew the elastic casing opening closed using whipstitch (see Techniques, page 116). Tie the ribbon in a bow and trim the ribbon ends on the diagonal to prevent them from fraying. Stitch the bow to the front of the waistband to finish.

appliquéd apron

This cute apron features a handy pocket and is adorned with an appliquéd initial – it makes a great gift or could be a crafting apron just for you!

YOU WILL NEED:

paper • scissors • pins • 60cm/24in fabric (137cm/54in wide) • 20 x 20cm/8 x 8in fabric for the initial • pinking shears • fusible web • contrasting coloured embroidery thread • 1.25m/4ft1in gingham ribbon (2cm/¾in wide) for straps

create templates Photocopy the apron and pocket templates on page 121 and cut them out. Pin the apron template to the back of the main fabric and cut around it using pinking shears. Turn in a 1cm/½in hem around the edges and ask an adult to help you press it flat using a hot iron. Sew it in place using running stitch (see Techniques, page 116).

appliqué initial Draw a large initial on a piece of paper then cut it out to use as a template. Iron the fusible web to the back of the initial fabric and allow to cool. Place the initial template on the paper side of the fusible web, draw around it and cut it out. Peel off the backing paper and position the initial on the front of the apron. Ask an adult to help you iron it in place following the manufacturer's instructions. Thread the needle with embroidery thread to work blanket stitch (see Techniques, page 114) all the way around the initial.

sew on pocket Turn in a 1cm/½in hem all around the pocket and ask an adult to help you press it flat with a hot iron. Pin the pocket to the front of the apron in the position indicated on the template and sew it in place using blanket stitch. Leave the top edge open but overstitch it with a row of blanket stitch to hold the hem in place.

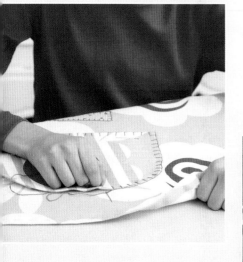

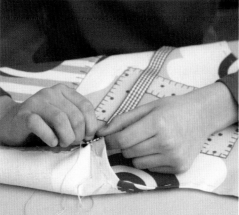

finishing Cut two lengths of ribbon measuring 45cm/18in. Sew the end of one piece to the side of the apron using whipstitch, and repeat with the other piece of ribbon on the other side of the apron. Cut a length of ribbon 35cm/14in long for the neck strap and stitch the two ends to the top two corners of the apron.

YOU WILL NEED:
1 pair old pyjamas • scissors
• pins • needle • sewing thread
• 1.2m/4ft rickrack

trim legs Cut the legs off the pyjama bottoms about 5cm/2in down from the crotch. Use sharp scissors and cut a curved shape at the outside of each leg.

hem edges On the first leg, turn up a double hem to hide the raw edge and pin it in place if necessary. Repeat with the second leg. Sew the hems in place using whipstitch (see Techniques, page 116), then ask an adult to help you press them flat using a hot iron. Allow the fabric to cool.

sew on trim Cut a length of rickrack and use running stitch (see Techniques, page 116), to stitch it around the first leg, about 5mm/¼in up from the bottom. When you have finished, fold the raw edge of the rickrack to the inside and finish with small whipstitches (see Techniques, page 116) to secure. Repeat on the other leg.

finishing Cut a length of rickrack measuring approximately 20cm/8in. Tie it into a bow and cut the ends on the diagonal to prevent them from fraying. Stitch the bow to the centre of the waistband to finish.

PJ shorts

Make these cute shorts from old pyjama bottoms and trim them with colourful rickrack and a ribbon bow.

fleece scarf

This cosy scarf decorated with pretty flowers is made from soft fleece fabric that does not require hemming as it doesn't fray, making it the ideal fabric for this project.

YOU WILL NEED:

20cm x 1m/8in x 3ft piece of
fleece fabric • scissors • paper
• 2 or 3 squares of coloured felt
for flowers • scraps of coloured
felt for flower centres • fusible
web • pins • needle • 3 buttons
(2cm/¾in diameter) •
contrasting embroidery thread

cut fabric and fringe Take the
piece of fleece and along the two shorter
edges, cut slits about 2cm/¾in apart to
create the fringing.

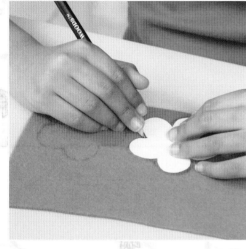

create template Photocopy the flower and circle template
on page 119 and cut it out with scissors. Ask an adult to help you
iron the fusible web onto the back of the felt for the flowers and
allow the fabric to cool. Place the flower template on the paper
side of the fusible web and draw around it six times. Cut out the
flower shapes.

cut out flowers Now place the circle template on the paper side of the
remaining felt scraps, draw around it and cut out six circle shapes.

finish flowers Peel off the
backing paper and position three
flowers at each end of the scarf. Ask
an adult to help you iron them in place,
following the manufacturer's instructions.
Using embroidery thread, blanket stitch
(see Techniques, page 114) around the
flowers. Stitch a felt circle and button to
the middle of each flower to finish.

YOU WILL NEED:

paper • scissors • pins • 30cm/12in fleece fabric (137cm/54in wide) • 3 or 4 squares different-coloured felt for flower and leaves • fusible web • 1 button (2cm/¾in diameter) • contrast embroidery thread • standard needle • large needle • double knitting wool

create templates Photocopy the hat, leaf, circle and flowers templates on page 119 and cut them out. Fold the fleece fabric in two, pin the hat template to the fabric and cut out two shapes. Now ask an adult to help you iron the fusible web to the squares of felt. Place the flower and leaf templates on the paper side of the fusible web and draw around them. You will need two leaves, one flower and one circle. Cut out the shapes. Peel off the backing fabric and ask an adult to help you iron the motifs to the front of the hat.

add decoration Work blanket stitch (see Techniques, page 114) all the way around the flower and leaf shapes and then firmly sew a felt circle and a button to the middle of the flower.

stitch hat Lay the two hat sections together with wrong sides facing and stitch all the way around the curved edges using blanket stitch and knitting wool.

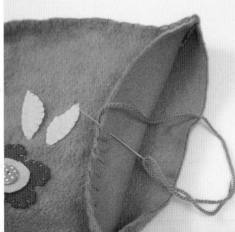

finishing Work blanket stitch along the bottom straight edge of the hat on the inside. Make a turning to the outside of the hat approximately 3cm/1¼in to create a fold and secure in place with a couple of stitches on both sides of the hat.

fleece hat

Make this cute matching hat to wear with your scarf – it's finished with a felt flower and leaves and edged in wool blanket stitch.

denim jacket

Personalise a denim jacket (either old or new) with a selection of beads and felt flowers to create this stylish fashion piece.

YOU WILL NEED:
denim jacket • small beads •
sewing thread • needle •
thimble (if required) • scissors •
2 large felt flowers • 4 flower-
shaped wooden beads

sew on beads Stitch the beads to the front seams of the jacket above the pockets at 1cm/½in intervals. You may need to use a thimble to push the needle through the fabric if the denim is very stiff.

sew flower beads to collar Stitch one of the flower-shaped beads to each side of the collar. Use a double layer of thread to make the beads more secure.

sew on felt flowers Sew two felt flowers to the front of the jacket just above the pockets, using blanket stitch or whipstitch (see Techniques, page 114 or 116).

finishing Stitch a flower-shaped bead to the centre of each felt flower. Sew a row of the small beads along the edges of the cuffs and the waistband of the denim jacket to finish.

accessories

YOU WILL NEED:

scissors • one pair old jeans • one back pocket from pair of kid's jeans • 4 assorted buttons (about 1cm/⅜in diameter) • needle • contrasting coloured embroidery thread • bobble trim to fit base of bag • sewing thread • 1m/3ft jumbo rickrack

cut fabric Cut the bag from the leg of the adult jeans. Cut straight across the leg at its widest point then cut across again 30cm/12in down. The existing seams will form the side seams of the bag. Now cut a pocket from the back of a pair of child's jeans. Cut as close as you can to the topstitching around the pocket so that the raw fabric edges do not show.

stitch on pocket Thread the needle and stitch the four buttons in place along the top of the jeans pocket. Now re-thread the needle with the embroidery thread and stitch the pocket to the front of the bag using blanket stitch (see Techniques, page 114).

attach bobble trim Make a 2.5cm/1in fold to the inside and ask an adult to help you press it in place with a hot iron. Cut the bobble braid to the length of the bottom of the bag and pin it along the bottom edge. Using running stitch (see Techniques, page 116), sew the braid in place. Make sure you cast off securely.

attach handle Use whipstitch (see Techniques, page 116) to stitch the ends of the rickrack to the inside of the bag beside the two side seams. Make sure you work a number of stitches so the bag handles are strong and secure enough for everyday use.

denim jeans bag

This cool shoulder bag is made from the leg of a pair of adult's jeans and decorated with a pocket cut from a pair of kid's jeans and a decorative rickrack strap.

stripy belt

This fun stripy belt is made from strong curtain braid decorated with coordinating buttons and finished with a smart silver buckle clip.

YOU WILL NEED:

Length of curtain braid to fit child's waist in trousers plus 4cm/1½in • interlocking metal belt buckle in two pieces • fabric glue • pins • strong sewing thread • scissors • thimble • approx 25 assorted buttons (about 2cm/¾in diameter)

thread braid Take one end of the curtain braid and thread approximately 2.5cm/1in through one piece of the belt buckle. You may wish to dab a small amount of glue on the end of the curtain braid to prevent the cut edges from fraying. Allow the glue to dry completely before beginning to sew.

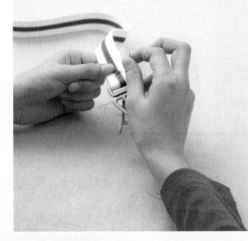

stitch in place Fold the braid back on itself and pin the end to the back of the belt then whipstitch it in place (see Techniques, page 116). You may need to use a thimble to help you push the needle through the braid.

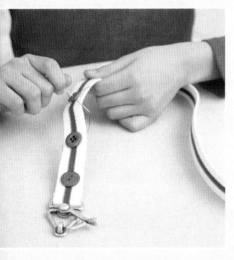

sew on buttons Stitch the buttons to the braid at regular intervals (ours are approximately 3cm/1¼in apart).

finishing Thread the other end of the braid through the second part of the belt buckle (glue the end as before, if required). Fold the braid back on itself and stitch the end in place at the back of the belt using whipstitch. Again, you may want to use a thimble to protect your fingers.

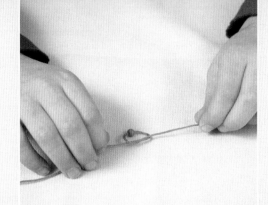

YOU WILL NEED:

**strong thread for threading
• 1 small wooden bead • large
needle for threading • 35
wooden beads • 9 felt flowers
• 5 felt beads • scissors •
15cm/6in narrow velvet ribbon**

knot end of thread String the small wooden bead onto the thread and tie in a knot at one end. This will prevent the beads from slipping off the end of the thread while you are stringing them.

thread beads Push the other end of the thread through the needle. Thread five of the wooden beads in assorted colours onto the necklace. It helps to have all the beads in front of you while you work, so you can choose which colour to thread onto the necklace next.

continue threading When you have added five wooden beads, thread a felt flower then a felt bead followed by another felt flower. Then thread another five wooden beads followed by a single felt flower. Now add another five wooden beads followed by a felt flower, bead and flower, and repeat until you have strung on all the beads and flowers. Leave approximately 8cm/3in of thread free at the end for tying the necklace.

finishing Tie the ends of the thread together in several strong knots then trim the ends with scissors. Tie the ribbon around the necklace and finish it in a bow. Trim the ribbon ends on the diagonal to prevent them from fraying.

bead
necklace

A combination of felt and wooden beads and felt flowers have been used to create this delightful necklace finished with a dainty velvet bow.

flower headband

This pretty headband is decorated with a rosette made from a length of floral fabric and finished with a sprinkling of tiny glass beads.

YOU WILL NEED:
50 x 6cm/20 x 2⅜in strip of cotton floral fabric • needle • sewing thread • scissors • 15 small glass beads • 40cm/16in length of coloured elastic (1cm/⅜in wide)

start sewing Take the long strip of fabric and start making tiny pleats in the fabric so it starts to curve into a circular rosette shape. Use running stitch (see Techniques, page 116) to stitch the pleats in place at the centre of the rosette as you work. Pull gently on the thread as you stitch to encourage the fabric to form a multi-layered circular rosette.

form rosette When you have finished sewing, carefully snip away some of the fabric edges on the top layer to create a pretty ruffled effect. If necessary, fray the edges of the fabric slightly.

sew on beads Thread the needle and use sewing thread to stitch the tiny glass beads to the centre of the rosette. Cast off securely when you have finished.

finishing Wrap the elastic around your head in the right position until you find a length that feels comfortable. Add 2cm/¾in to this length then cut the elastic to size with scissors. Stitch the two ends of the elastic together, overlapping them by 1cm/⅜in. Securely stitch the flower rosette to the elastic to finish.

YOU WILL NEED:

25 x 25 cm/10 x 10in square of fabric for pocket • needle • embroidery thread • 20 x 20cm/8 x 8in gingham for initial • fusible web • paper • pencil • scissors • 1m/3ft fabric (137cm/54in wide) for main bag • pins • 1.4m/4½ft cotton cord • 6cm/2¼in gingham ribbon (2cm/¾in wide) • safety pin

make pocket Take the square of plain fabric for the pocket. Fold the four edges 1cm/½in to the inside and ask an adult to help you press them flat with a hot iron. Allow the fabric to cool then sew along one edge using running stitch (see Techniques, page 116). This will be the top, open edge of the pocket.

stitch initial to pocket Iron the fusible web to the back of the piece of gingham. Draw your chosen initial on a piece of paper then cut it out to use as a template. Place the initial template on the paper side of the fusible web and draw around it (remember that you will need to reverse non-symmetrical initials when drawing them on the back of fabric). Cut out the initial. Peel off the backing paper and position it in the middle of the pocket. Ask an adult to help you iron it in place, following the manufacturer's instructions, and allow to cool. Now work blanket stitch (see Techniques, page 114) all the way around the initial.

sew on pocket Cut a piece of fabric measuring 60cm/2ft in length. This will form the body of the duffle bag. Pin the pocket to the centre front of the fabric then sew it in place using blanket stitch.

sew side seam Fold the piece of fabric in half with the right sides facing. Pin if necessary then stitch all the way along the long edge using back stitch (see Techniques, page 116) and working 1cm/½in from the raw edge. Leave a 2.5cm/1in opening about 6cm/2½in down from one end of the fabric – this is where you will insert the drawstring cord.

duffel bag

This handy duffel bag is useful for holidays, to hold swimming kit or as an overnight bag for sleepovers!

sew base to bag Cut out a circle of 22cm/9in diameter from the bag fabric. This is the base of the bag. Place the circle on the bottom of the bag, right side facing in. Fold the gingham ribbon in two to form a loop, then insert it between the bottom of the bag and the bottom piece, making sure the loop is facing towards the inside of the bag and the ends are between the two pieces of fabric. Stitch the base to the bag using back stitch.

make casing for cord Turn the top edge of the bag 3cm/1¼in to the inside and ask an adult to help you press it flat with a hot iron. Allow the fabric to cool then turn the bag right side out and stitch the top seam in place using running stitch (see Techniques, page 116). Leave the sides of the seam open so you can insert the drawstring cord.

insert the cord Wrap a small piece of sticky tape around one end of the cord to prevent it from fraying and attach the safety pin to this end. Insert the cord into the casing through one of the open ends of the seam at the top of the bag. Use the safety pin to chase the cord all the way through the casing and out through the other end.

finishing Remove the safety pin and thread one end of the cord through the gingham ribbon loop. Now tie the cord ends together in a secure knot. Trim the ends of the cord, leaving approximately 2cm/¾in at each end. Fray the ends of the cord by hand.

YOU WILL NEED:

oval box approximately 22 x 17cm/9 x 7in diameter • pink paint • paintbrush • 25 x 25cm/ 10 x 10in square of felt • scissors • glue • 6 small felt flowers • 12 beaded motifs for lid • 20 assorted small buttons • 1.2m/4ft velvet ribbon (2cm/¾in wide) • 60cm/2ft narrow rickrack

paint box Paint the lid and the box inside and out and allow to dry. You may want to apply another coat of paint for complete coverage. Place the lid on the square of felt and draw all the way around it. Cut out the felt oval and glue it to the lid of the box. Allow to dry.

decorate lid Use glue to stick the felt flowers and beaded motifs at equally spaced intervals around the lid of the box. Stick a heart-shaped button in the very centre of the lid and place six beaded motifs around the button. Allow the glue to dry.

attach rickrack Wrap the velvet ribbon around the rim of the lid and cut to the correct length. Glue the ribbon around the rim and let it dry. Cut a piece of rickrack to the same length and glue this on top of the velvet ribbon. Leave to dry.

finishing Wrap a length of velvet ribbon around the base of the jewellery box and cut to the correct length. Glue the ribbon all the way around the base, about 1cm/½in up from the bottom, and leave to dry. Glue the buttons on top of the ribbon at regularly spaced intervals to finish.

treasure box

This fun painted keepsake box is decorated with ribbon and rickrack as well as beaded felt flowers and buttons. It's a good place to keep your most treasured possessions!

braid bracelets

Use a length of pretty ribbon or braid and decorate it with felt flowers and beads to make a lovely bracelet or two.

YOU WILL NEED:

15cm/6in velvet ribbon
(2cm/¾in wide) • 15cm/6in
narrower ribbon or rickrack
(1cm/½in wide) • needle
• sewing thread • scissors
• 20cm/8in ribbon for ties
(1cm/½in) • 1 felt flower •
4 beaded motifs • glue

sew on ribbon Lay the narrower ribbon or rickrack on top of the velvet ribbon, making sure it is positioned right in the middle. Use running stitch (see Techniques, page 116) to sew the narrow ribbon in place. Cast off securely when you have finished.

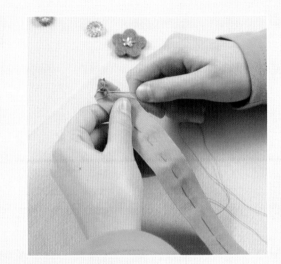

fold corners Working at the ends of the ribbon, fold the ends into the back diagonally, so that a small triangle is formed at each end. Use tiny whipstitches (see Techniques, page 116) to secure the folded ends in position. Repeat at the other end.

sew ribbon ties Cut the 20cm/8in of ribbon in half and pin one piece to each end of the bracelet, folding the ends 1cm/½in towards the inside. This will cover the raw edges of the folded velvet ribbon. Whipstitch in position.

finishing Turn the bracelet to the right side and glue the felt flower to the middle of the bracelet. Then stick beaded motifs either side of the felt flower at evenly spaced intervals. Leave the glue to dry completely to finish.

YOU WILL NEED:

2 pieces felt measuring 33 x 25cm/13 x 10in for the bag • 2 strips felt measuring 4 x 40cm/1½ x 16in for the handles • 60cm/2ft jumbo rickrack • contrasting coloured embroidery thread • needle • scissors • squares of felt for the leaves and pot motif • 60–70 assorted small buttons • pinking shears

sew on buttons Photocopy the pot and leaf templates on page 120 and cut them out. Place the templates on the felt squares, draw round them and cut out a pot and two leaves. Position these on the front of the bag then use blanket stitch (see Techniques, page 114) to sew them in place. Start sewing the buttons to the front of the bag in the shape of a large circle about 2cm/¾in above the felt pot.

stitch bag together When you have finished sewing on the buttons, place the front and back bag sections together with wrong sides facing and stitch around three sides using running stitch (see Techniques, page 116). Leave the top edges of the bag open and sew a line of running stitch along these edges to match the sides of the bag.

trim edges When you have finished sewing the bag, carefully trim the sides and top of the bag using pinking shears to create a decorative finish. Be careful not to cut through any of the stitching.

sew on handles Using the pinking shears, trim the strips of felt for the handles. Pin the rickrack to the middle of each strap then sew it in place using running stitch. When you have finished, stitch the handles to the inside of the front and back of the bag, about 5cm/2in from the sides. Cast off securely when you have finished.

button bookbag

A selection of buttons in assorted shapes and sizes are used to create the design on this felt bookbag. If you want to make the project easier, simply glue the buttons to the front of the bag rather than sewing them in place.

hair scrunchies

Make these fun scrunchies using
scraps of fabric and elastic – you
can create ones to match your
favourite outfits and even your
school uniform!

YOU WILL NEED:
Strip of fabric 36 x 10cm/
14 x 4in per scrunchie •
scissors • 22cm/9in elastic
(8mm/⅜in wide) • sewing
thread • needle • safety pin

start sewing Take the strip of fabric and fold it in half lengthways with right sides facing. Starting approximately 3cm/1¼in from the end, stitch a 1cm/½in seam using running stitch (see Techniques, page 116). Stop stitching 3cm/1¼in before you reach the the other end of the fabric. This leaves an opening to thread the elastic through.

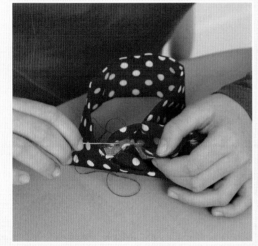

sew side seams Turn the tube of fabric right side out. Tuck in the raw ends then fold over the tube so the folded ends meet, and stitch them together using running stitch. Do not sew up the opening along the long seam of the scrunchie.

insert elastic Attach the safety pin to one end of the elastic. Insert the elastic into the scrunchie through one of the openings on the long seam. Chase the elastic all the way through the casing and out the other end. You may find it easier to pin the other end of the elastic to the fabric as you are threading.

finishing Remove the safety pin once you have finished threading and stitch together the ends of the elastic using whipstitch (see Techniques, page 116). Now fold the open edges of the scrunchie to the inside and whipstitch the opening closed to finish.

YOU WILL NEED:
paper • scissors • pencil
• squares of felt in 3 different
colours • felt glue • button
(about 2cm/¾in diameter)
• needle • thread • metal
brooch back

cut out shapes Photocopy the
flower template on page 120 and cut it
out. Each brooch requires two flowers
and one circle. Place the template on the
felt and draw around the flower twice. Cut
out carefully with scissors. Cut out one
circle shape for each brooch.

form flower Lay one felt flower on top of the other so that the
petals are staggered and then lay the felt circle on top in the
middle of the flowers. Add a dab of glue between each layer of felt
to keep them in place.

stitch together Place the button right in the middle of the felt circle and stitch it
to the felt through all three layers. Cast off securely to hold the layers in place.

finishing Turn the brooch to the wrong
side. Spread a line of glue along the metal
brooch back and stick it in place on the
back of the flower, pressing down firmly
to finish. Allow the brooch to dry before
you wear it.

felt flower brooches

Colourful felt flowers are layered together and finished with a button to create funky badges.

blanket stitch

Blanket stitch is usually worked in wool to finish the raw edges of a blanket or wool fabrics. It is a pretty, decorative stitch that is useful for creating a bold outline. Use tapestry or knitting yarn for this stitch.

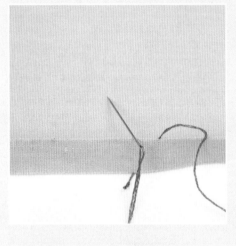

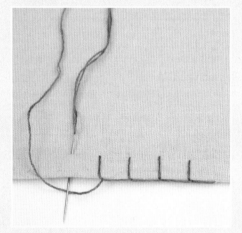

1 Fold up the raw edges of the fabric approximately 1cm/½in to the inside. Press in place if necessary. Now push the needle through the fabric from the wrong side so it emerges from the folded crease. Carefully pull the needle all the way through.

2 Next, push the needle through the front of the fabric, about 1cm/½in along from the previous stitch or at the distance stated in the step by step instructions. Pull the needle out through the fold of the hem with the thread looped underneath the point of the needle. Pull the thread through.

3 Repeat the stitch, always remembering to loop the thread under the point of the needle to create the blanket stitch. Take care not to pull the thread too tight. Always keep the stitches evenly spaced – it is best not to work them too far apart.

cross stitch

This stitch is worked in two parts and is great for filling in large expanses. It is possible to buy woven fabric (usually sold as Aida or Evenweave) with holes spaced especially for cross stitch. Alternatively, it works well on fabrics with woven or printed designs of square or checks, such as gingham.

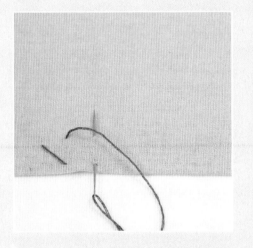

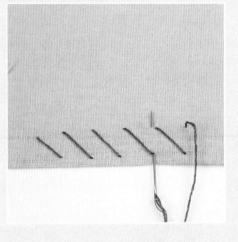

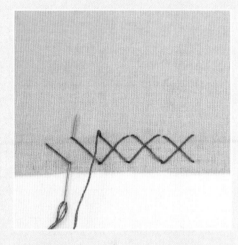

1 Cross stitch is generally worked in rows. Knot your thread and push the needle through from the back of the fabric to the front. Make a diagonal stitch downward from right to left and then push the needle back up to the top of the line of embroidery. Repeat for the desired number of rows.

2 When the length of the first line is completed, the stitch is reversed to form the crosses that give the stitch its name. Pass the needle back across the first stitch on a diagonal from left to right. Push the needle through the fabric at the bottom of the line of the embroidery to form an X.

3 Continue to pass the needle neatly and evenly through the fabric on a diagonal, until you have formed an entire row of stitches. Repeat the process until you have built up the desired number of rows.

running stitch, back stitch and whipstitch

These simple but essential stitches are essential for every budding stitcher and are all easy to master. Try practising them on scraps of fabric before starting a project.

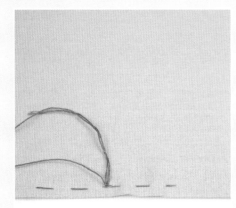

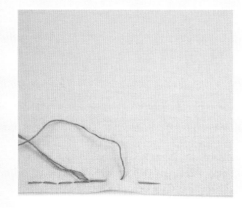

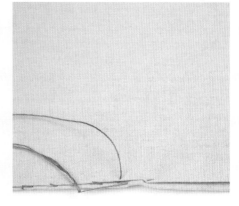

Running stitch This is a series of small, straight stitches that are equal in length on both sides of the fabric. Thread the needle and work from the edge of the fabric pushing the needle through the fabric from front to back and then pushing the needle back through to the front of the fabric again.

Back stitch Thread the needle and work from the edge of the fabric – push the needle through from the back of the fabric to the front. Rather than pushing the needle in front, put it back behind where it was to create a stitch approximately 8–10mm wide. Repeat by pushing the needle back through the fabric as you work the stitch to create a neat line of stitches that resemble a line of sewing machine stitches with no gaps.

Whipstitch This stitch is for neatly sewing openings closed and joining together two layers of fabric. Work on the wrong side of the fabric. Start with a knot and the needle in the fold. Push the needle through the two layers from back to front and pull the thread through. Insert the needle into the hem again and make another stitch about 5mm/¼in from the first. Continue making stitches and cast off with a few close stitches.

templates

The outlines shown on pages 118–123 have been reduced in size so they fit on these pages. Before cutting out the templates, you must enlarge them on a photocopier by 200 per cent to make them the right size.

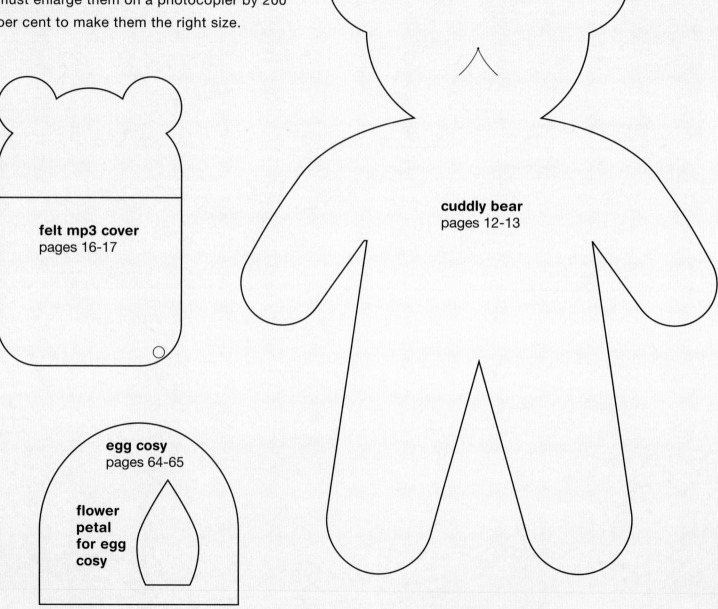

felt mp3 cover
pages 16-17

cuddly bear
pages 12-13

egg cosy
pages 64-65

flower petal for egg cosy

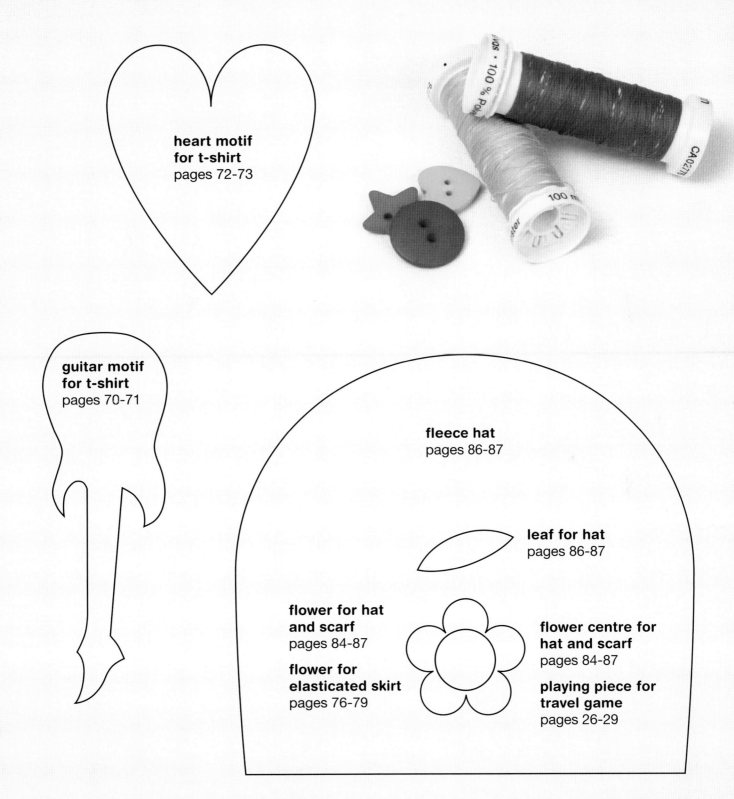

**heart motif
for t-shirt**
pages 72-73

**guitar motif
for t-shirt**
pages 70-71

fleece hat
pages 86-87

leaf for hat
pages 86-87

**flower for hat
and scarf**
pages 84-87

**flower for
elasticated skirt**
pages 76-79

**flower centre for
hat and scarf**
pages 84-87

**playing piece for
travel game**
pages 26-29

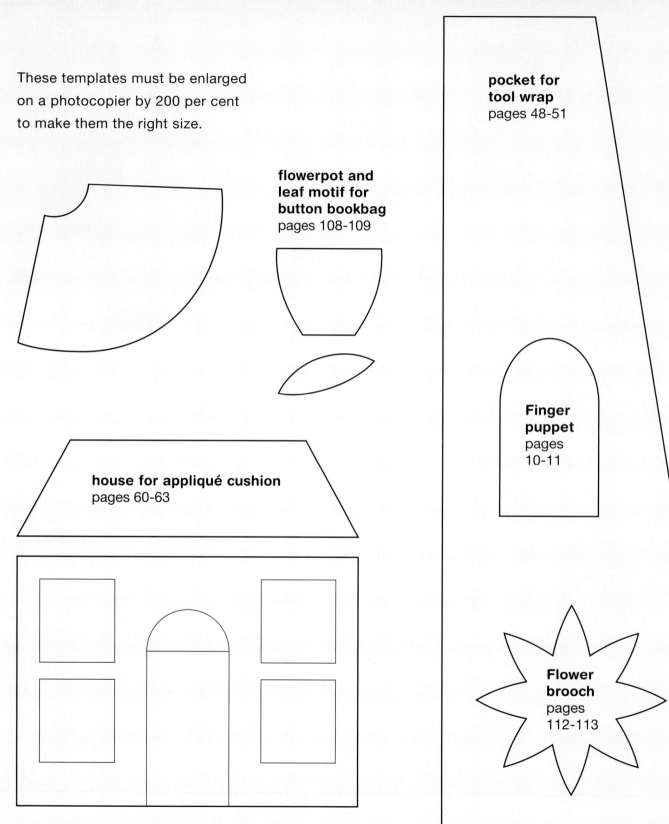

These templates must be enlarged on a photocopier by 200 per cent to make them the right size.

flowerpot and leaf motif for button bookbag
pages 108-109

house for appliqué cushion
pages 60-63

pocket for tool wrap
pages 48-51

Finger puppet
pages 10-11

Flower brooch
pages 112-113

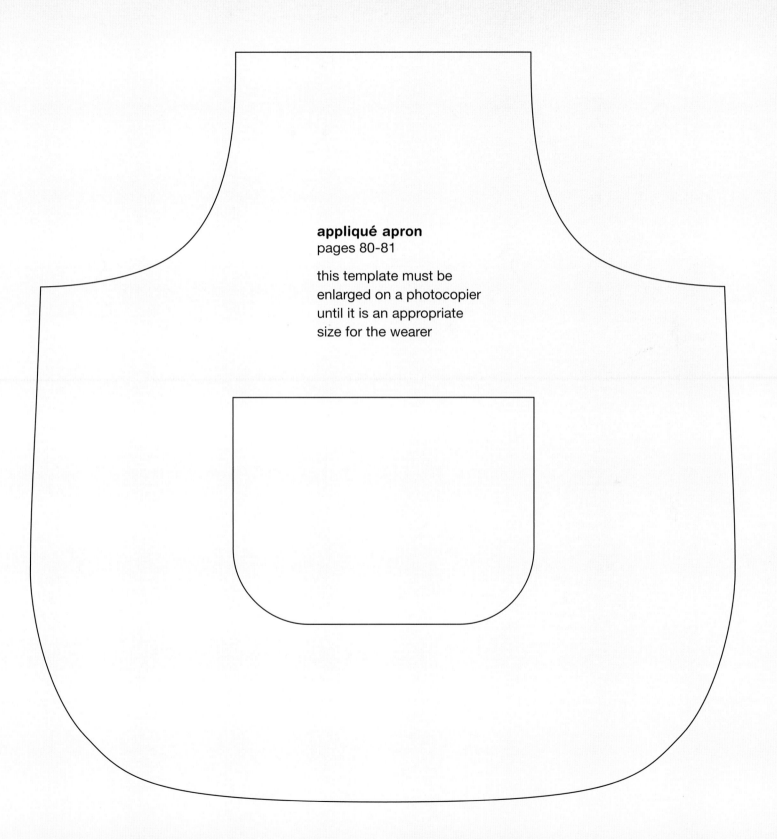

appliqué apron
pages 80-81

this template must be
enlarged on a photocopier
until it is an appropriate
size for the wearer

This template must be enlarged on a photocopier
by 200 per cent to make it the right size.

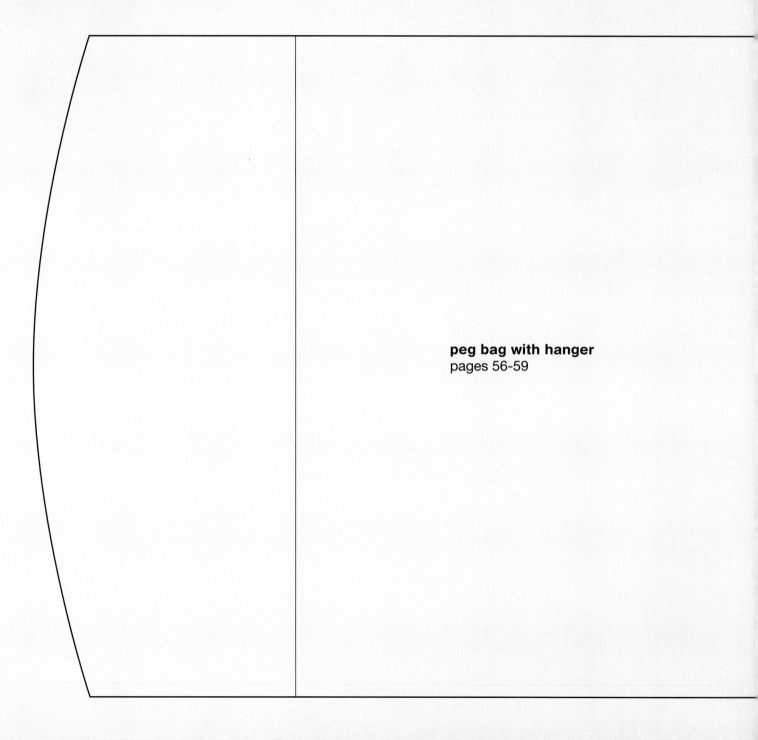

peg bag with hanger
pages 56-59

UK sources

BEADWORKS BEAD SHOP

21a Tower Street

London WC2H 9NS

0207 240 0931

www.beadworks.co.uk

Glass beads, pearls, rocailles and bugle beads plus findings and jewellery tools.

THE BUTTON QUEEN

76 Marylebone Lane

London W1U 2PR

0207 935 1505

www.thebuttonqueen.co.uk

Buttons from pearl and wood to colourful plastic. They also offer a button-covering service in a wide range of designs using your own fabric.

CALICO CRAFTS

www.calicocrafts.co.uk

Online crafts specialist with large haberdashery section and useful fabrics including calico and gingham.

CALICO LAINE

0151 336 3939

www.calicolaine.co.uk

Fleece fabric, felt, trims, coloured elastic, braid,

fusible web, googly eyes, gingham, craft materials, embellishments and general haberdashery.

CREATIONS ART AND CRAFT MATERIALS

01326 555777

www.ecreations.co.uk

Online craft store with large stock of buttons, decorative fabric motifs, cord, ribbon and elastic, and fabric paints as well as all the usual sewing accessories.

THE ENGLISH STAMP COMPANY

01929 439117

www.englishstamp.com

Rubber stamps that can also be customised to include your child's name or address. From simple designs to more complex motifs, the selection is comprehensive and available in different sizes. Also stocks a good selection of coloured stamping inks.

HOBBYCRAFT

Westway Cross Shopping Park

Greenford Road

London UB6 0UW

0845 0516528

www.hobbycraft.co.uk

Chain of craft superstores carrying embroidery thread, sewing accessories, ribbons, haberdashery, fusible web and a wide selection of decorative buttons.

HOMECRAFTS DIRECT

0116 269 7733

www.homecrafts.co.uk

Sewing motifs, fancy threads, ribbon and braid, fancy trims, glass, wooden and plastic beads and brooch backs as well as fleece fabrics and felt.

IKEA

Visit www.ikea.co.uk for a catalogue or details of your nearest store.

Wooden boxes and files and plain picture frames for decorating or decoupaging as well as a good selection of furnishing fabrics.

JOHN LEWIS

Visit www.johnlewis.com for details of your nearest store.

The store's haberdashery department stocks a good

range of buttons, rickrack and ribbon plus all the usual sewing accessories.

SEWING AND CRAFT SUPERSTORE
296–312 Balham High Road
London SW17 7AA
0208 767 0036
www.craftysewer.com

Everything from beads and sequins to fusible web, brooch backs, polyester toy stuffing, googly eyes and beaded motifs.

THE STENCIL LIBRARY
Stocksfield Hall
Northumberland NE43 7TN
www.stencil-library.com

Great selection of stencils from simple designs to large complex motifs. They also supply a good range of fabric paints and brushes.

VV ROULEAUX
261 Pavillion Road
London SW1X 0PB
0207 730 3125
www.vvrouleaux.com

Ribbons, rickrack and braids in silk, cotton and velvet plus embroidered motifs and fabric flowers.

US sources

A.C. MOORE
Call 866-342-8802 or visit www.acmoore.com for your nearest store.

Craft superstores carrying polyester toy stuffing, notions, ribbons, sewing supplies, embroidery thread, stencils, wooden clothespins, and embroidery hoops.

BRITEX FABRICS
146 Geary Street
San Francisco, CA 94108
415-392-2910
www.britexfabrics.com

Ribbons, décor trims and tassels, and notions.

THE BUTTON EMPORIUM & RIBBONRY
1016 SW Taylor Street
Portland, OR 97205
503-228-6372
www.buttonemporium.com

Vintage and assorted decorative buttons.

HEART OF THE HOME STENCILS
www.stencils4u.com
888–675–1695

Alphabet stencils as well as other simple designs for kids.

HOBBY LOBBY
Visit www.hobbylobby.com for your nearest store.

Fleece and calico fabrics as well as children's prints. Also sewing supplies, notions, ribbons, trims and buttons.

HYMAN HENDLER & SONS
21 West 38th Street
New York, NY 10018
212-840-8393
www.hymanhendler.com

Novelty and vintage ribbons.

IKEA
Visit www.ikea.com/us for your nearest store.

Unpainted wooden photo frames, plain tins for découpaging, and cute accessories.

JO-ANN FABRICS
Locations nationwide. Visit www.joann.com for your nearest store.

A wide selection of sewing supplies.

KARI ME AWAY
www.karimeaway.com

Rickrack and bobble trims in a large variety of colors. Also novelty buttons and glass beads.

MICHAELS
Visit www.michaels.com for your nearest store.

Every kind of fabric craft material, including beads, fabric paints, embroidery thread, yarns, glues, and elastic.

M&J TRIMMING
www.mjtrim.com

Fancy trims, including rhinestones, sequined flowers, ribbons, lace, rosettes, beaded braid, and fur and feather trims.

THE RIBBONERIE
3695 Sacramento Street
San Francisco, CA 94118
415-626-6184
www.ribbonerie.com

Extensive collection including wired, grosgrain, metallic, and velvet ribbons.

TINSEL TRADING CO.
1 West 37th Street
New York, NY 10018
212-730-1030
www.tinseltrading.com

Vintage buttons and beads, as well as gorgeous silk and velvet flowers, sequins, metallic tassels, and exquisite ribbons.

picture credits

page 2–3 Gingham fabric, embroidery thread and buttons from The Sewing and Craft Superstore; cushion pad from John Lewis; metal bed and duvet cover from IKEA. **4–5** Felt fabric, rickrack, embroidery thread and buttons from The Craft Superstore; small felt flowers from VV Rouleaux. **6–7** Oval card lidded box, velvet ribbon and wool felt flowers from Hobbycraft; star-print fabric, gingham ribbon, buttons, floral fabric, dotted fabric, embroidery hoop and fleece fabric all from The Sewing and Craft Superstore; apron fabric and boat print fabric from John Lewis; rickrack and beads from The Sewing and Craft Superstore. **8–9** Gingham fabric, wool fabric, felt, knitting wool, braid, elastic and buttons from The Sewing and Craft Superstore; wooden pegs, dotted felt and narrow rickrack from Hobbycraft; socks from H&M. **10–11** Plain and dotted felt fabric and knitting wool from Hobbycraft; 3-D fabric pens, wooden buttons and rickrack from The Sewing and Craft Superstore. **12–15** Wool fabric, polyester toy stuffing and embroidery thread from The Sewing and Craft Superstore; floral fabric from Hobbycraft. **16–17** Felt fabric, self-adhesive googly eyes, pompom and embroidery thread from The Sewing and Craft Superstore. **18–19** Stripy socks from H&M; buttons, polyester toy stuffing and knitting wool from The Sewing and Craft Superstore. **20–21** Wooden pegs and narrow rickrack from Hobbycraft; PVA glue, 3-D fabric pens, floral fabric and paint all from The Sewing and Craft Superstore. **22–23** Wooden pegs, and narrow rickrack from Hobbycraft; PVA glue, 3-D fabric pens, floral fabric and paint all from The Sewing and Craft Superstore. **24–25** CD case from John Lewis; skull-and-crossbones fabric, buttons, poppers and googly eyes, rickrack and glue from The Sewing and Craft Superstore. **26–27** Stiff calico fabric, felt, glue and fabric paint all from The Sewing and Craft Superstore; stencil brush and masking tape from Hobbycraft. **28–29** Stiff calico fabric, felt, glue and fabric paint all from The Sewing and Craft Superstore; stencil brush and masking tape from Hobbycraft. **30–33** Duktig dolls bed from IKEA; gingham, dotted and striped fabric, braid, polyester stuffing and cotton thread all from The Sewing and Craft Superstore. **34–35** Gingham fabric, felt, calico and striped fabrics, rickrack, buttons, felt flowers, fabric paint all from The Sewing and Craft Superstore; boat stencil from The Stencil Library; cushion pad from John Lewis; bandana from Bandanashop.com. Blank card and wool pompoms from Hobbycraft. **36–37** Bandana from Bandanashop.com; PVA glue and embroidered initials from Hobbycraft; notebook from Paperchase. **38–39 and 40–41** Dotted fabrics and felt flowers from The Sewing and Craft Superstore; cushion pad from John Lewis. **42–45** Calico fabric, fabric paints and rickrack from The Sewing and Craft Superstore; stencil brush from Hobbycraft; boat stencil from The Stencil Library. **46–47** Gingham fabric, embroidery thread and fabric paint from The Sewing and Craft Superstore. **48–51** Felt fabric, embroidery thread, fusible web and gingham ribbon from The Sewing and Craft Superstore. **52–53** Star-print fabric, wadding and gingham ribbon from The Sewing and Craft Superstore; drawing pins from Hobbycraft.

54–55 Gingham fabric, embroidery hoop and embroidery thread from The Sewing and Craft Superstore; blank card from Hobbycraft; pearl button from John Lewis. **56–59** Striped fabric, felt flowers and buttons from The Sewing and Craft Superstore; braid from Hobbycraft; small wooden hanger from John Lewis. **60–63** Gingham fabric, fusible web, button and embroidery thread from The Sewing and Craft Superstore; cushion pad from John Lewis. **62–63** Felt, embroidery thread and wool pompoms from Hobbycraft. **64–65** Fleece fabric, fusible web, embroidery cotton and wool thread from The Sewing and Craft Superstore; boat print fabric from John Lewis. **66–67** Felt flowers and wood beads from Hobbycraft; denim jacket from Gap; fleece fabric, elastic and buttons from The Sewing and Craft Superstore; dotted fabric from IKEA. **68–69** Star-print fabric, buttons, fusible web and embroidery thread all from The Sewing and Craft Superstore; long-sleeved t-shirt from H&M. **70–71** Floral fabric, miniature buttons, fusible web and embroidery thread from The Sewing and Craft Superstore; long sleeved t-shirt from H&M. **74–75** Rickrack, buttons and small glass beads from Sewing and Craft Superstore; jeans from Gap. **76–77 and 78–79** Pink dotted fabric from IKEA; red dotted fabric, elastic, dotted ribbon, fusible web and buttons from The Sewing and Craft Superstore. **80–81** Embroidery thread, fusible web and gingham ribbon from The Sewing and Craft Superstore; dotted fabric from IKEA; printed apron fabric from John Lewis. **82–83** Rickrack ribbon and cotton thread from The Sewing and Craft Superstore. Pyjamas from Primark. **84–87** Fleece fabric, felt, embroidery thread and buttons from The Sewing and Craft Superstore. **88–89** Felt flowers and wooden beads from Hobbycraft; denim jacket from Gap. **90–91** Felt fabric, buttons and spotted fabric from The Sewing and Craft Superstore; lidded box, velvet ribbon, wooden beads and wool beads and flowers all from Hobbycraft. **92–93** Bobble braid, buttons and rickrack from The Sewing and Craft Superstore. **94–95** Striped curtain braid, buttons and belt buckle from The Sewing and Craft Superstore. **96–97** Velvet ribbon, wooden beads, thread, wool beads and flowers all from Hobbycraft. **98–99** Beads, thread and elastic from The Sewing and Craft Superstore; floral fabric from Cath Kidston. **100–103** Boat print fabric from John Lewis; red fabric and gingham, rope cord, embroidery thread and fusible web all from The Sewing and Craft Superstore. **104–105** Oval lidded box and beaded felt flowers from Hobbycraft; rickrack, felt and buttons from The Sewing and Craft Superstore. **106–107** Velvet ribbon, rickrack and gingham ribbon from The Sewing and Craft Superstore; felt flowers, beaded motifs and glue from Hobbycraft. **108–109** Felt fabric, rickrack, embroidery thread and buttons from The Craft Superstore. **110–111** Dotted fabric and elastic from The Sewing and Craft Superstore. **112–113** Felt fabric, buttons, brooch back and glue all from The Sewing and Craft Superstore.

index

acknowledgments

Thank you very much to Penny Wincer for her wonderful photography, enthusiasm and great ideas for shooting the book. Thanks also to Annabel Morgan and Sonya Nathoo for their help at all stages of the book – with design, layout and words.

Thank you also to Hobbycraft for supplying their fun felts and fabrics as well as buttons and trims and thank you to The Stencil Library for the boat stencil.

Thank you to my daughter Jessica for designing the flower hairband and to my youngest daughter for allowing us to "borrow" her legs for the elasticated skirt photograph.

Finally, a big thank to my husband Michael for his help and patience as well as suggestions for this latest book.

Ryland Peters & Small would like to thank the lovely models that appear in this book: Anna, Blaise, Celia, Charlotte, Emma, Elisha, Honor, Immy, Izzy, Julian, Lauren, Lily, Maddie, Oliver, Omar, Peter, Polly, Sean, Tilum and Zain.